To Don,
Best Wishes!
Jerome Ait

Also by Jerome Arthur

Antoine Farot and Swede
Down the Foggy Ruins of Time
Life Could be a Dream, Sweetheart
One and Two Halves
The Journeyman and the Apprentice
The Muttering Retreats
The Death of Soc Smith
Oh, Hard Tuesday
Got no Secrets to Conceal
Brushes with Fame

The Finale of Seem

A Novella

Jerome Arthur

The Finale of Seem

Published by Jerome Arthur
P.O. Box 818
Santa Cruz, California 95061
831-425-8818
www.JeromeArthurNovelist.com
Jerome@JeromeArthurNovelist.com

Dedicated to Janet

Acknowledgments
Special thanks to Don Rothman for his
invaluable editorial assistance.
Cover design by Jim Mullen.

One

"What a day!" I said to Betty as we went down the mountain on our way home. "I've got this one mother who just keeps trying to run my classroom, and she's been doing it all year. She keeps making suggestions on what I should teach and how I should be teaching it. You know how I adapted *Tikki Tikki Tembo* to put on this Friday for my classroom play?"

"Yes?"

"She suggested I use *Winnie the Pooh* instead."

"Oh, Lord!"

"And that isn't the first time she's tried to tell me how to teach a class. I want to ask her exactly where she got her teaching credential, but I never do."

The Finale of Seem

We'd just come around the bend and saw the panoramic view of the ocean that we got every time we made that drive. That was last year, and a lot's happened since then. Betty and I are still making the drive, but the town's in trouble, and it looks like it's going to last for quite a while. In October we had the Loma Prieta earthquake. It was a seven on the Richter scale, and it shook the foundations of our little town. Our house made it okay, but most of downtown was wiped out. Buildings that weren't demolished in the quake later met their fate at the hands of the wrecking ball. We still don't have full access to downtown. But that disaster was nothing compared to the one I met just four months earlier.

When we got down to the highway, I turned left and went south into town. The neighborhood was quiet as it usually was on Monday afternoon. I pulled up next to Betty's car. She got into it and drove away. Then I pulled into the driveway, got out of the car and opened the garage door. I noticed Soc's car wasn't there, so I just assumed he'd gone surfing again. I pulled my car into the garage and closed the door. I went out the side door and across the patio to the back door of the house. I set my tote down on the dining room table, and while unpacking it, I noticed the note. Soc's handwriting. I picked it up and read:

Honey,

I'll be gone by the time you get home today. I love you. Remember that always. I just can't stay here any longer. I don't know what to do to get my life back. I guess, nothing, so I'll just be on my way. I must be dead. I love you.

Soc

My first reaction was anger, but it quickly turned to hurt feelings. Tears welled up in my eyes. What was going on? Was Soc really gone? Was this a suicide note? I went into our bedroom and checked the closet. All of his dress clothes were still hanging on the rod. His casual clothes, pants and sport shirts, were all missing. The same for the drawers where he kept his shorts, T-shirts and underwear. They were empty. So was the cup that held his toothbrushes, and the drawer with the toothpaste and dental floss. When I saw all that, I knew it wasn't suicide.

Back in the dining room, I looked at the note again. I didn't know what I expected to find in those few words of farewell, but I was looking for a clue, any clue, that would tell me where Soc had gone. I wanted to go and look for him. I wanted to kill him. Not literally. It was like when Caroline was little, and I would say something like, "I could kill you," when she did something I told her not to do.

An ominous thought occurred to me at that moment. What if he really was dead as he had said in the note? I didn't actually believe it was a suicide note. I wasn't ready to think that Soc could do something like that. What if it was a prophesy rather than a simple statement? What if he'd been killed by some other means? What if he'd had a blow-out along the coast and was down in one of those ravines that go under the highway and the railroad tracks to the beach in Santa Barbara? The thought lingered, and then I wondered if it was possible to live without him, which would be the case if he was dead. Scary thought. I didn't want him to be dead. I wanted to get him back, and I'd make sure his voice was higher when I got him here. Of course, I'm only speaking metaphorically. I was really more interested in getting our lives back to normal. But right in that moment, I really did want to kill him. How could he do this?

I went into the living room and sat down on the couch to think. Our problems started when that obituary was published in the newspaper the Saturday before last. The whole week that followed, our lives were hell. Soc was moody, and he acted disoriented all week long. And when I got home that Monday afternoon, my husband was gone. Disappeared. He was certainly suffering more than I was, and that made complete sense. After all, his life was affected more directly than mine.

The Finale of Seem

I had to decide what to do to find him, how to track him down. Who did he talk to in the last week before he left? I thought of following that path, and I could start doing it the very next day. I'd take a personal leave day and go to all the places Soc told me he'd gone to the Monday before. Talk to those people. See if he mentioned to any of them what his plans were.

As it turned out, my actual search would have to wait a couple of months for school to get out. That would be the soonest I'd be able to do it, the soonest I'd be able to find someone to help me. And I knew who that person would be, a good friend of mine from school, Danielle Bourdain. She'd been my aide a few years back. When she left, she took a job teaching in a nursery school downtown. She and her husband, Jason, didn't have any kids. He worked for a start-up company in Silicon Valley. We remained friends over the years. We'd probably gone out to lunch at least once a month since she'd been working downtown. Danielle was always a lot of fun to be around. Both of us had the same kind of sick sense of humor.

12

I went to the front door to get the mail. There were no clues among the assorted bills due and junk mail ads. I went into the bedroom, sat down on the bed and sobbed uncontrollably. After about five minutes of crying and then laughing, I finally pulled myself together and started thinking about a plan. When I thought about it, this was all really quite humorous. Then I suddenly remembered the money we kept in the file cabinet. The last time we both looked together, there were twenty-five thousand dollars in there. I took out my key and unlocked the bottom drawer. In the back there were three envelopes, each with five thousand dollars in hundreds. We'd just checked it the week before when the trouble started, and there were five envelopes. That thieving sack of shit! Well, at least he left me more than he took. I was prepared to spend it all looking for him.

I got up and went back to the kitchen. As I was passing the full-length mirror on the wall in the hallway, I stopped. I turned on the light and looked at myself. Even with my eyes red from crying, overall I saw a handsome woman in the looking glass. In fact, the crying eyes made me look kinda' cute. Younger even. Although, cute wasn't really the word I'd have used to describe myself. That's mostly because of my height. I'm hardly what you would call petit. I've been five-eight since sixth grade, and I've weighed about a hundred and forty-five pounds since sophomore year in high school. As I looked at myself in that mirror, I thought what a good-looking woman I was with my graying auburn hair and blue eyes. I wasn't a classic beauty by any means, but I've always been attractive, and, with my sense of humor, it's what Soc called the full package. I went into the dining room and looked at Soc's note again.

How could he have done what he did and think he'd get away with it? My mind was made up. I'd find him and make him pay. When all was said and done, we'd had a good life together, and I really couldn't see any reason why it couldn't continue. I was going to make myself something to eat, and then I'd sit down and make up my list of things to do. One thing I'm really good at is organizing my thoughts, writing them down, and formulating a plan, and there's always a plan B. So that's what I started to do.

I went into the kitchen and made a salad, another one of my specialties. When Soc and I were first married, he was always complimenting me on my salads. He would tell me how good they were, and they were, but I like salads more because they're good for my health, and good for my figure. Now, just for plain good flavor, I'd rather have a medium rare steak and baked potato dripping sour cream and chives. That might be the best tasting thing on earth. I like mine bloody. But I could only eat that kind of a meal every once in a while. If I did it even once a week, I'd gain weight, and I didn't want to do that.

After I finished eating, I washed the dishes and cleaned up in the kitchen. I took the phone and my address book into the dining room. I looked up Danielle's phone number and dialed. She picked up on the third ring.

"Hi, Danielle," I said.

"Jayne, hi, how are you?"

15

"Not good."

"Oh? What happened?"

"Remember what we talked about on Saturday at lunch?"

"Yes, Soc's obit? What about it?"

"I'll read the note he left this morning after I went to work," I said and read the note to her.

"Noo!" she said in that incredulous way she had of saying it. "What happened?"

"I honestly don't know. This whole situation has obviously been bothering him a lot. It's bothered me too, but I've thought from the beginning that we'd get it straightened out. Apparently, he didn't. Well, he's not getting out that easily. I wan'a find him and bring him home. You wan'a help?"

"Tell me what you want and I'll do it."

"First thing I'll do is take the day off tomorrow and trace his footsteps from last Monday. See if he left any clues to where he might've gone. If I find out anything, I'll think seriously about hiring a private investigator. To be honest with you, I think he might've gone to Baja California. Over

16

---

the years, he's talked about Baja with a certain wanderlust gleam in his eye. I know my man."

"Boy, you sure are easy to forgive."

"I wouldn't go that far. I haven't found him, yet. When I do, I may be singing a different tune."

"Have you thought that he might be dead? Suicide comes to mind."

"I've definitely considered that possibility, but I just don't think so. It's completely out of character for him. Besides, he took clothes and toiletries with him. I guess it's possible that he might die before we get to him. Like maybe he could run off the road before he gets to where he's going, or if he's heading for México, I suppose he could be held up and killed by banditos. But I'm not worried about suicide. I'm going looking for him, and the search starts tomorrow."

"You want me to go with you? I can take the day off, too."

"Actually, no. Tomorrow's just the beginning. I was thinking more like summer when school's out. Think Jason'll let you get away for a while?"

The Finale of Seem

"It's not a question of him 'letting' me do anything. If I want to, I'll go. How long you think we'll be gone?"

"I have no idea. I may know more after I find out where he is. I just can't say for sure."

"Okay. Just let me know. The earlier the better, so I can arrange for a couple days in our timeshare in Las Vegas. If we're going to Baja, Vegas is kinda' on the way. We may as well stop there. Do a little gambling. Have some fun. You deserve a treat after what that man is putting you through."

"Absolutely, and a couple of days in Las Vegas sounds like fun. You've just made my day a lot better than it was a little while ago."

We hung up. I made one more call to Margot, my regular sub. She said she could cover for me, and I briefly told her what my lesson plan was. After we hung up, I sat down and had another good cry at the dining room table. Then I started making plans.

Two

I was up at six o'clock the next morning as usual. I made the bed and got into the shower. The phone rang right after I got into the tub, and then it rang again when I turned the water off. Drying myself, I could see my reflection once again in the hall mirror through the open bathroom door, only this time I was naked, and once again, I couldn't help but admire what I saw. I straightened up and took a good look. Not bad for fifty-one. Boobs were sagging a little, not quite as perky as they once were, but everything else looked trim and firm. Flat stomach and firm glutes. For my age my skin was pretty smooth and supple. Jazzercise every Saturday at the roller rink was paying off.

The Finale of Seem

I got dressed and went to the kitchen to make breakfast. Before I started it, I checked the phone messages. The first one was from Caroline, the second from LaVerne. After I got the coffee started, I went out to the front porch and picked up the newspaper. I spread it out on the dining room table, and poured myself a cup of coffee. Then I made myself a bowl of oatmeal and toasted a half slice of whole wheat bread. I read the paper and ate.

At seven o'clock I called school and left the message that I wouldn't be coming in, and that Margot would be subbing for me. Then I reviewed my list of things to do. I'd go to the county first. That's where Soc had started. Instead of the newspaper, I'd go see our lawyer Rob Novak next, since his office was a short walk from the county building. I'd have to call first to make sure he'd be there. If Soc said anything to anybody about where he was going, Rob would have been the one. The only other one I could think of was Roland. I'd check with him, too. Maybe later on. After those two stops, I might not have to make the others if I got any solid clues from them.

I still had another half hour before I'd be leaving, so I went about returning the phone calls on the answering machine. I wasn't going to get back to Caroline right away. I had to think about it before I told her what was happening. I responded to LaVerne's call. She picked up on the first ring. I told her the whole story: how when I got home from school on Monday and found Soc's note, and then I read it to her.

"What is going on?" she asked.

"I'm not quite sure myself. I'm going to go check at the county and the newspaper to see if he said anything to anybody there about what his plans were. I'm also going to talk to Rob, his oldest friend. He's known him since college in Long Beach. He's a lawyer. I might have better luck with him."

"I can't believe this. You know how much I've always liked Soc. I just can't believe he'd do something like this. What was he thinking?"

"I don't know, Hon'. What time is it? Oh, hey, it's eight o'clock. I've got to get off the line. Got'a call Rob. Find out if he has time to see me today."

"Okay, Darlin', but you be sure to tell me if there's anything I can do."

"I will. 'Bye."

"'Bye."

I thought about having LaVerne go with me on the search, but I knew she wouldn't. Even though *her* husband, Chuck, was always away traveling on one adventure or another, she would never think of doing that herself. She just wouldn't.

I dialed Rob's number and he picked up.

"Hello, Rob?"

"Yes."

"Oh, hi. This is Jayne Smith. Surprised you answered the phone."

"Oh, yeah. Hi Jayne. My receptionist doesn't come in till nine. That's when I'm off to court. What can I do for you?"

I read him the note, and asked if he had any idea where Soc might've gone.

"God, Jayne, not really. I know he always seemed enamored of Baja, but I can't say for sure that's where he might've gone. Wow! This just absolutely blows my mind."

"It is strange, isn't it?"

"How soon can you be here? I've got an idea, but I don't want to talk about it on the phone."

"Ten minutes," I said and hung up.

It was eight-thirty when I drove into Rob's parking lot. His car was the only other one there. As I walked through the front door into the reception area, he came out of the door to his private office.

"Hi, Jayne. Come on back."

He held the door for me, and I went in and sat down in the chair facing his desk. Leaving the door open, he went around the desk to his chair and sat down.

"After you hung up, I called a private investigator I use. He's on his way. I think he may be able to locate Soc, wherever he might be. This guy's really good at finding people."

"Good. So, Soc didn't say anything to you about any of this?"

"Nope. In fact, I thought he seemed pretty positive and upbeat when he left here last Tuesday. Confident it'd get straightened out. I know I was, and I tried to convey that to him. This comes as a complete surprise to me. Never thought he'd just disappear."

"Me either. Me least of all."

The front door opened, and Rob shifted his glance from me to the outer office.

"Hey, Jack. C'me on back here."

Coming through the door was a tall, good looking guy who resembled Jim Rockford in looks and in his demeanor.

"Jack Lefevre, this is Jayne Smith."

I stood up and shook his hand.

"Why don't you two go into my library where you can have some privacy?" Rob said. Then to me, "I gave Jack a brief review of the situation."

Jack and I moved off to the small library next to Rob's inner office.

"So, explain to me exactly what happened. Rob just gave me a brief sketch over the phone."

I took Soc's note out of my purse and handed it to him. Then I went on to tell him everything that had happened to us in the ten days before. I handed over copies of the newspaper obituary, the county death certificate, and the cover letter and the $50,000 check I received from the life insurance policy.

"And you don't have a clue where your husband might've gone?" he asked after looking over the documents.

"My guess would be Baja California. Over the years, he's talked about that place a lot.

"Rob told me he was a fan. Think he might've gone there?"

"It's a good possibility. I can't think of anywhere else. He's driving his old woody, and he took his surfboard and wetsuit, so I know he's gone somewhere that has surf and he can get to in an old car."

"He ever talk about anyplace specific that he liked down there?"

"We only visited there a couple times in the twenty-five years we've been married. Once to Tijuana before Caroline was born and once to Ensenada a few years ago, but he didn't particularly care for either of those two places. Too lowbrow touristy for either of our liking, and too dumpy."

"I understand that. Did he ever talk about any other places?"

"Not really. Maybe Hawaii, but he couldn't drive there and he's terrified of flying. Another one might be Costa Rica, but that's a long way to go in his old car. Baja would be too far for that matter. By the way, how much will you be charging me for your services?"

"You'll need to pay me two thousand dollars to get started. That'd be a thousand for a retainer, and a thousand for expenses. My normal fee is two-fifty a day plus expenses. If it takes more than five days, I start charging you the two-fifty plus, and it's go'n'a take me at least that long. Maybe longer. First thing I'll need is a picture of Soc and his car. You'll also need to give me a list of his friends. You know, his surfing buddies and anyone else he hung around with? Meantime, I'll talk to as many surfers as I can who go down to Baja a lot. Find out where the best breaks are. You think Soc'd be looking for the best spot he'd ever heard about?"

"Absolutely. You find out where the best break is, and that's where he'll be. I guarantee it."

"Okay, I'll get started as soon as I receive the first payment, the photo and the list of names."

"We can take care of the money and picture right now if you'll just follow me home. I only have the first names of his friends at Cowell's. One he mentions a lot is Jesse. I think his heritage is Filipino. He's the only one I've met. He should be easy to find at Cowell's at low tide."

"I'll have to get my longboard out. Go out at Cowell's this afternoon."

"You're a surfer?"

"Yeah. I kinda' like Middle Peak at the Lane when it's happenin'. Been out at Cowell's a couple times. Always fun...."

"It's the only place he surfs, and the way he talks, it's the only one any of his friends surf. Favorite one for most of 'em, anyway. I'll put Roland's name on the list, too. He's Soc's best friend. They golf together."

27

The Finale of Seem

"What's your address? I'm go'n'a have to swing by my place on Center Street before I go up to your house."

I gave him our address and phone number and we left. I got to the house enough before him to go get some of the money we had in the file cabinet in our closet. After I got twenty one-hundred dollar bills out of the cash, the front doorbell rang. I went out and greeted Jack. We went to the dining room table, and I gave him the money. He'd brought a contract with him, and as he wrote out a receipt, I made a list of Soc's surfing friends and took a picture out of one of my albums. It was a great shot of Soc standing next to his woody in his wetsuit holding his board straight up next to him. He'd just gotten out of the water at Cowell's. I'd gone down one day and watched him from up on the cliff. I took another picture as he got to the top of the steps, but that one didn't have the car in it. I also gave Jack a head shot. I briefly reviewed the contract and signed it. He gave me the pink copy and kept the original.

"I'll get started on this right away. I'll give you a status report at the end of each day that I work on the case. You'll be hearing from me around five o'clock."

He left and I called Caroline. Her answering machine picked up. I left her a message to call me back. I wanted to tell her what was happening directly. I didn't think it would have been appropriate to leave her a phone message about something this important. After all, her father had abandoned her, too. That's pretty scary.

After lunch I drove out to Triple A and got a map of Baja California. When I got back home, I spent about a half hour perusing the map. I couldn't tell much from looking at it. I put it away and spent the rest of the afternoon weeding the flower beds in front. I'd learned long ago that the best therapy in these kinds of situations was to work in the garden.

Three

Jack called me at five o'clock. I was just finishing up in the garden. He told me he'd talked to a couple of Soc's friends at the beach and to Roland.

"Guys at Cowell's weren't too eager to tell me anything," he said. "Acted like they didn't know much. Roland didn't know much either. He did say the same thing you and Rob said about him going to Baja. I talked to a guy who works in the surf shop down by the beach. He goes surfing in Baja a couple times a year. Said he's surfed every break down there."

"Wait a minute. After you left this morning, I went to the Auto Club and got a map of Baja California. I'll go get it."

I went into the bedroom and got the map from the dresser.

"Okay I've got it spread out."

"Guy I talked to said it's hard to tell which is the best break in Baja. There're so many good ones. One spot he goes back to a lot is called Santa Rosalillita, halfway down the peninsula. You see it on your map?"

"Yes!" As soon as I found it, my instinct told me that's where Soc had gone. "God, that looks just like a place he'd go to."

"Definitely a good possibility. Your map's just like mine. You can see that the town's toward the end of a group of points. Together they're all called Seven Sisters. If you look closely, it looks like two of those points are accessible from a gravel road. The rest only have dirt roads or no road. How adventurous is Soc? Would he be likely to take his car out on a dirt road given how old it is?"

"He could. That old car is in good shape, but I don't know if it's *that* good, or if he'd be willing to do that."

"Okay. Here's my plan. I'm go'n'a fly to San Diego, rent a four-wheel drive

31

vehicle and a surfboard. Drive to Santa Rosalillita. Branch out from there. Check out the Seven Sisters. See if that's where he went. Right now I'm go'n'a make some phone calls. Reserve my plane tickets and rent-a-car. I'll set it all up for a couple weeks from now. If Soc just left yesterday, it's go'n'a take him a couple/three days to get there."

"Oh, it'll take him longer'n that. He'll probably check every surf break between here and there."

"Okay. All the better. It gives us some time. You said this morning you wouldn't be able to go looking for him till your school term ended. Right?"

"Right."

"When'll that be?"

"Another six weeks."

"Okay, so we've got a couple weeks to get started. Right?"

"Yes, I think so."

"I'll call you before I leave."

"Great."

We hung up, and I sat by the telephone for a while. I thought about the situation, and the more I thought, the angrier I got. I started to question my own motives. Why was I even going looking for the jerk? If he could leave as easily as he did after all those years, what kind of a man was he? Maybe it wasn't worth doing. But I was going to do it, and I was going to have some fun with Danielle along the way. Besides, the house was entirely too quiet without him in it.

I called Danielle to let her know what was happening. Then I went back out to the flower beds in front and packed up my weeding tools and the bags of weeds I'd been filling throughout the afternoon. I emptied the bags in the green recycle and put the tools away.

When I came back into the house, I thought it was time to talk to Caroline. She hadn't returned the call I'd left her earlier. It was eight-thirty East Coast time, and she was in her dorm room studying for a test she had the next morning. I told her the whole story from when I got home yesterday till when I just talked to Jack moments ago. When I finished, she burst into tears. She was having

33

a complete meltdown, sobbing and carrying on. I started crying too. It surprised me because I didn't think I had any tears left after Monday. Understandably, this was a big deal for both of us, but her tragic/romantic personality was really coming out then. I never understood why Caroline was so insecure. She worried about everything, and there usu-ally was no reason for it. Most of the time I thought she overreacted, but this time she had a point. It took me ten minutes to calm her down, but even then she wasn't completely pacified. Then she asked me, her voice rising, if it was possible that her dad might have committed suicide.

"No!" I said emphatically. I wasn't eager for her to start carrying on again. "I thought of that possibility at first, but I put it out of my mind. Your father is not suicidal. He is many things, but not that."

I think I would have said anything to keep her from going back into hysterics. I could almost feel her stress traveling through the phone line, and it was increasing my own.

"You know, Mom, I'm scared."

"As you should be. I'm scared too, but I'm more angry than anything. We've just got to buck up.

Finally I got her calm, but before we hung up, she argued that she wanted to go with Danielle and me to look for her dad.

"No," I said. "I don't think you should change a routine that you've been fol- lowing since you moved to the east coast. I think you should go to the Christian conference center you've worked at every summer since you got there."

"I wan'a come home instead and help you look for Dad. I couldn't possibly stay here knowing what you're going through out there."

"Well, you'll have to, 'cause what I have to do, you can't be a part of. This is something between your father and me. You'd be more help working and earning money to help with your tuition. I'll call you as often as I can when I'm on the road. I don't know if I'll be able to do it when we're in México, but I'll most certainly call when we get to Las Vegas. That'll be our first day out."

The Finale of Seem

"W'll, okay, but it'll be hard."
"I know, Hon. You'll survive."
And with that we hung up.

*　　*　　*

It was two weeks before I heard from Jack Lefevre again. He called on Sunday to tell me he was getting ready to fly to San Diego.

"I'm leaving here tomorrow morning at nine. Probably won't get into San Diego till about noon. It's a little over four hundred miles from there to Santa Rosalillita. You got your map handy?"

"Hang on." I got the map and spread it out on the table. "I'm ready."

"You see Camalú? Couple hours down the road from Ensenada? Near the beach?"

"Yes."

"Go'n'a try to make it that far the first day. Don't wan'a be traveling after dark down there. Should be able to hit Santa Rosalillita next day. I'll call you before I leave

San Diego, and then you won't hear from me again till I get back there."

"That'll be fine."

Now I would just have to wait. And wait I did. Jack called and left a message on my answering machine at a little after noon. He'd gotten a car earlier and had just then rented a surfboard and was getting ready to drive into México. He said he would call me when he got back to San Diego, and then he hung up.

The next time I heard from him was Thursday afternoon. He was at the airport in San Diego getting ready to catch a flight home. He said he'd be home by seven o'clock, and he'd be at my house by seven-thirty. He arrived at seven-twenty. I poured him a cup of coffee, and we sat down at the dining room table with the map spread out.

"I found him," he said after he took a sip of coffee. "He was exactly where you thought he'd be after you saw Santa Rosa-lillita on the map." He pointed to it. "It's a little town sitting right on the beach. Can't be more'n a couple hundred people living there. Probably the biggest one of the Seven

The Finale of Seem

Sisters. A cantina, a church. Prob'ly less than a hundred houses and trailers. And when I say houses, I don't mean like what you have here. The ones I'm talking about are more like shacks. You can see here that it's the only one that has a gravel road to it and it's the closest one of the Sisters to Highway 1. I spotted his car right away when I got into town. Parked next to a trailer. I drove straight down to the beach and looked at the surf. Didn't wan'a look like I was there for anything other than surfing. There was one guy in the water. Pretty good swell comin' through. Found out later it was Soc."

"Did you see him, talk to him?"

"No I didn't. Didn't want to. I was actually pretty lucky. I went into the bar and asked the bartender who owned the forty-eight Chevy Woody. He mentioned a name, not Soc's, but he said the owner only came to town about a week ago. It was his car. Looked like the one in the picture. Same license plate. Bartender told me he was the one in the water. Soon as I heard that, I drove right straight back out of town and headed north. I don't think it would've been a good idea to meet him. It might've scared him away if he thought he was the reason I was there."

"I understand," I said.

Jack completed his report, and we settled accounts. He recommended that I rent one of those small S.U.V.s like he did to drive on the Mexican roads. I thought that was a good idea and planned to do it. I thanked him and he left. Then I called Danielle and told her everything I'd learned in the report. We both only had a few weeks left of school, so we tentatively planned our trip for one week after school got out. I hung up, content in the knowledge that I had a plan and a friend to help mc carry it out.

Four

The rest of the school year was uneventful. My kids put on the class play the next day after Jack gave me his report, and the mother who suggested the other play said the one we did was good, but she would rather I'd done the one she wanted to do. Boy, was I ever ready for the school year to end.

And end it did a couple of weeks later. Thursday was our last day of classes; sixth grade graduation was on Friday. Danielle and I decided to leave the following Monday. I'd go to Budget car rentals on Sunday, get the S.U.V. and be ready the next morning. After the last time I spoke to Jack, Danielle'd reserved her timeshare in Las Vegas for Monday and Tuesday nights. My plan was to leave there early Wednesday and drive to San Diego. We were going to take this trip in style. I reserved a room at the Hotel del Coronado on Coronado Island. It was expensive, but worth every penny. Growing up, Caroline became an early fan of Marilyn Monroe, and her favorite Marilyn movie was *Some Like it Hot*. Almost all of it was filmed in and around that hotel. When Caroline was ten years old, we took a trip to La Jolla, University City actually, where my mother-in-law lived. We spent a couple of hours one afternoon visiting the Hotel del. Caroline was absolutely enchanted by the experience.

The plan was to get on the road early Thursday after a night on Coronado, and try to make it to Camalú, the same town where Jack said he stayed. Then hopefully we'd get into Santa Rosalillita sometime Friday afternoon, barring any delays along the way.

Jack described the motel he stayed in, and it sounded okay. Camalú is only a couple miles from the beach, and Jack said it looked like it's ripe for development. He said there were only a couple very modest motels in

41

The Finale of Seem

town. We found out later that his description was accurate. Very modest. Rustic was more like it. He said when he'd gone into the first one, he waited around in the office for ten minutes, and no one came to help him. He finally left when he couldn't find anyone to rent him a room. He went to the next one and someone was there, so that's where he stayed.

We wanted to get an early start so Danielle got to my house at seven o'clock. We were on the road by eight, heading down Highway 1 to Salinas. I wondered if this was the way Soc had gone. I was sure it was.

"I just don't get why Soc did this," I said as we were leaving town. "I mean it's not as though I was stepping out on him. Actually, quite the opposite is true. He's the only one I've ever been with."

"Really?"

"Yup."

"Unbelievable. But then again not so much. You *are* such a nice, decent person, one of the nicest I've ever known."

"You're too kind."

"No, it's true. Look how polite you are to those crazy parents you deal with at school."

"You have a point there. But you know, you have to be polite in that job. It would be unprofessional if I didn't show some common courtesy."

"That's true. But I live in that community, and, believe me, I know how crazy they are. That's the main reason I left that school and went to work downtown. It was too close to home."

"You also went from part-time aide to full-time teacher, don't forget."

"Yes, I did. But getting away from that community a few hours a day was a big factor. So, is it really true you've never slept with anyone but Soc?"

"That's right."

"Like my sister. She's probably only ever slept with her husband. Now I, on the other hand, have had a little more experience. My sister's more like you. Married to the same guy forever. Teenagers when they tied the knot. Got two grown kids. Neither one of 'em has slept with anybody but each other."

43

The Finale of Seem

"How do you know that?"

"You can tell. Believe me, when you've had as much experience as I've had, you can tell."

"I guess you're right, but I don't notice things like that. Sex isn't a big deal with me. I like it; I'm just not one who dwells on it."

"Me too, really. I've had my share, so it just doesn't seem so important anymore. I was a virgin all the way through high school. The first time I got laid, I couldn't see what the big deal was, but after I did it a few times, I couldn't get enough."

"I remember that feeling. I had it after the first time Soc and I made love."

"But then after doing it a few times, it got to be like anything else that you do over and over again."

"Exactly."

"You really start to discriminate. Now I wouldn't think of having sex with anybody but Jason. Otherwise, you only fantasize about it. Know who I dream about sexually"

"Danielle!" My tone was more surprise than judgment. "I'm dying to hear!"

"Mike Wallace. Now that's my idea of a real hunk. You see *Sixty Minutes* last night?"

"I was busy packing for the trip."

"It was a rerun that I've seen before. He nailed some guy who was defrauding Medicare. That's when he's the sexiest, when he's catching people lying. I never get tired of watching Mike Wallace trapping the bad guys."

"I guess."

We kept going down the road and got on Highway 101 in Salinas at about nine o'clock. It took us another two hours to get to Paso Robles. We got off the highway on Spring Street and drove into town. We stopped at a restaurant called Wilson's to have an early lunch. It was a real, old-fashioned diner with leather upholstered booths and matching stools that made a wavy line along a shiny, curving Formica counter.

The waitress who served us had some pins and buttons on the bib of her apron. They were military insignia, a parachute with wings, a couple of eagles, silver and gold oak leaves, etc. My guess was that she'd gotten them over the years from customers who'd been stationed at Camp Roberts and Fort Hunter Liggett just a little north of there. I didn't ask her, so I never found out for sure where they had all come from. This was a really old, established coffee shop. I could see where soldiers from far away would want to come to a place like Wilson's. The food was good, and for a lot of those soldiers, the restaurant was probably a lot like something from back home.

We both had caesar salads. Danielle is like me when it comes to watching her figure. She's slim and trim and watches what she eats. She's ten years younger than I. That age was when I was at my sexual peak. Who knew, maybe we'd get hit on in Las Vegas. Wouldn't that be wild? Having my first affair after twenty-five years of marriage, and after my husband had left me. Not.

We finished lunch and got back on the road. We took State Highway 46 east to I-5. Just past Cholame we saw a monument off on the side of the road.

"There's the memorial to James Dean," I said. "This is where he died."

"Yes, I know. Jason and I stopped here once on our way to Las Vegas and looked at it. He's a big James Dean fan."

"It's been over thirty years since that fateful day."

"Doesn't seem possible it was that long ago."

"I know."

We drove on to Lost Hills where we got onto I-5 south. At Buttonwillow we got on State Highway 58 and took it through Bakersfield and up over the Tehachapis to Barstow. From there it was a straight drive on I-15 to Las Vegas. At this point in the trip, I was sure glad the car I'd rented had air conditioning. It was unbelievably hot on the Mojave Desert.

"Yuh know, when I was a little girl, my parents used to take us on trips to Las Vegas," I said, "and it was so hot that the road ahead used to shimmer just like it's doing now, and Daddy would say, 'You could fry an egg out there on that pavement.'"

47

The Finale of Seem

"I believe it's true."

We drove past the "Entering Fabulous Las Vegas" sign at about seven-thirty. It was still over a hundred degrees. The drive was long and we were tired, so we went straight to Danielle's timeshare, which was in a place called Royal Vacation Suites near the Stardust Hotel.

Five

After we checked in and got settled in our room, we called room service and ordered sandwiches and a couple glasses of wine. When we finished eating, Danielle got in the shower. I sipped my drink, called Caroline and brought her up to date. After Danielle came out, I took a quick shower too. We finished our drinks, got into our bathing suits and the terry cloth robes provided by the timeshare and went down to the pool.

It was as dark as it ever got in Las Vegas at nine-thirty at night, what with the neon lights and all, and the temperature was still ninety-five degrees. It was delightful in the pool. For about fifteen minutes, we were the only ones there. Then two young guys showed up. One of them was a pretty good diver. He immediately went to the board and started doing some fancy dives. The other one was doing laps. Next a family, a couple with two kids, came into the pool area. Danielle and I got out of the water and relaxed on a couple of chaise lounges.

The young man who'd been diving got out of the water and came over to sit in the lounge next to mine. The other one stayed in, swimming laps. Both of them were really in good shape. Swimmers' bodies. Big shoulders, narrow waists. In fact, I thought at the time that the one doing laps was actually doing a workout, trying to keep in shape for some future event. When the diver got close enough, I could see how young he was. I guessed mid thirties, but he looked much younger than that.

"Hi, my name's Chad," he said as he sat down. "You ladies been in Vegas long?"

"Just got into town couple of hours ago," Danielle said. "You?"

"We been here a couple days. Be leaving day after tomorrow. On our way to Salt Lake to visit friends. We live in Pasadena. Where you ladies coming from?"

Jerome Arthur

"Santa Cruz, California."

That was my first contribution to the conversation. If I'd been with anyone other than Danielle, I probably would have been the first to say something to the young man. I was always talking to strangers anywhere I went. Soc made fun of that part of my personality. I never heard the end of it the time we got our car towed on Sunset Boulevard. One night we drove from Long Beach, where we were living at the time, up to Hollywood to see the John Cassavetes movie, *Faces*. We didn't see the no parking sign, so we went ahead and parked, and when we came out of the movie, our car was gone. We called the number on the sign and went over to where they had towed it. We didn't bring enough money to get it out, so we called my parents, and my dad came over and bailed our car out. While we were waiting for Daddy to get there, I struck up a conversation with a man standing out on the sidewalk. As far as I was concerned, he was just a nice man who wanted to talk, but Soc told me later in the car going home that he was a wino, and he was surprised the man didn't ask me for some spare change. After he said that, I realized he was probably right. Every time after that when I'd start talking to a stranger, Soc'd rib me about that incident.

"Oh, really. Santa Cruz's a nice town. Me and Jerry went to school at San José State," he said, gesturing to the other young guy in the pool doing laps. "Went there to be close to the Santa Clara Swim Club where we trained with George Haines. We'd go over the hill to Santa Cruz all the time."

"Did you, now?"

"Yeah. Great surfing in Santa Cruz."

"Boy, do I ever know that."

"You surf?"

"No, but my husband is avid."

"R'illy? He surf the Lane?"

"He likes Cowell's."

"Where's that?"

"Know the Dream Inn?"

"Yeah."

"That's Cowell's. My husband says that's the break for little kids and old men, like him. He says the Lane's for really good surfers. Pros."

"How old is he? Can't be *that* old?"

"Fifty-three, two years older than I."

"Wow! I don't believe it. You look a lot younger'n that."

"Thank you. Such a sweet thing to say."

"I'm serious."

Just about then the other fellow got out of the pool and came up behind him.

"Serious about what, big brother? Since when did you get serious about anything?" he said jokingly.

"This is my little brother, Jerry." He then turned to me and said, "What're your names?"

I hesitated a moment, debating whether or not I should give these strangers my name, but they seemed to be such nice, normal young men that I went ahead and said,

"I'm Jayne and my friend here is Danielle. Nice to meet you boys."

"Nice to meet you," Danielle said.

I immediately regretted calling them boys because that was the same as them calling us girls, and I really didn't like it when men referred to women as girls. Although, I *was* getting to an age where it was kind of nice to be thought of by any man, no matter how young or old, as a girl.

"How long you ladies lived in Santa Cruz?" Chad asked.

"Soc and I moved there in 1969 from Long Beach."

"My husband, Jason, and I got there ten years after Jayne and Soc."

"That's an interesting name, Soc. What's it short for?"

"Socrates."

"Interesting. I remember reading parts of Plato's *Apology* in college. It's all about a Greek philosopher and teacher named Socrates."

"That's who Soc was named after."

"So, what do you ladies do in Santa Cruz?"

"We're teachers. I'm second grade; Danielle's preschool."

"Yuh know," Danielle said, "we just finished another long hard year in the grind. Think we could talk about something else?"

54

"Oh, absolutely," said Chad. "We're teachers too, and I'd just as soon talk about anything other than work."

"Actually, I think we should go up to our room," I said to Danielle. "We had a long drive today, and I can hardly keep my eyes open this late."

It *was* getting late. We'd been at the pool for about forty-five minutes.

"I suppose you're right."

"It was nice meeting you fella's. Maybe we'll see you tomorrow if you're still go'n'a be here for another day."

"Hey, we'll look for yuh."

We left them at the pool, and as we entered the building, I turned and saw Chad walking to the diving board and Jerry getting back in the water. When we got to the room, we got ready for bed, and then we talked before we fell asleep.

"What nice young men Chad and Jerry were," I said.

"Yes, they were. I think they were flirting with us."

The Finale of Seem

"Oh, no question. I especially felt that kind of a vibe coming from Chad. I'm just not interested in getting involved that way."

"You should be! After what you've been through with that husband of yours. How long's it been since you've seen him? A couple months? Did he tell you where he was going? NO! I don't see where you've got any obligation to him at all."

"It's tempting, but I'm just not interested in youngsters like Chad and his little brother. My God, I must be old enough to be their mother. They're nice enough boys, and sexy to be sure, but they just don't turn me on. Know how I told you how Soc was the only one I've ever made love with? Well, there's a reason for that. I don't think I'll ever meet anyone who'll excite me the way Soc does. I can't explain it any other way."

With that, we fell asleep, and I had an ominous dream. I dreamed I found Soc and when I did, he was already with another woman. She was a young and beautiful Mexican girl with long black hair and dark eyes, but when I got a closer look, her eyes had changed color and were blue.

"Sorry, Hon," Soc said in the dream.

"Is that all you have to say," was my reply.

He seemed so happy and content. I started to cry. He tried to comfort me, but I would not be comforted. I suddenly felt abandoned and alone. I didn't know where Danielle was. She wasn't in the dream. I cried some more. It felt more like I was whimpering. Someone had me by the shoulder and was nudging me awake. It was Danielle.

"You okay?" she said as I awoke.

"I think so," I replied tearfully. "I just had a scary dream."

I described it to her, and she comforted me in a way that Soc couldn't do in the dream.

"Hey, like Dylan said in 'Talking World War III Blues,' '...them old dreams are only in your head....' Don't take it seriously."

Six

When I made up my mind to go on this journey, I decided to take the fifteen thousand dollars from the closet with me. I hadn't cashed the life insurance check because I knew I'd have to return it when this mess with Soc got cleared up, as I knew it would. I took the cash to the bank and exchanged it for travelers checks. I didn't care if I spent it all. You can bet Danielle and I were going to have a good time. And too bad about Soc. After all he *did* abscond with ten thousand of it. And it wasn't the money. Far more disheartening was that he left. And for my part, I wasn't going to gamble all of the money away in a casino. I was going to spoil myself shopping. With that in both our minds, Danielle and I thought we'd go over to Caesars Palace first, see what it was like, maybe treat ourselves to some of the things we wouldn't otherwise indulge in. So the first thing we did after we woke up the next morning and got dressed for the day was to go have breakfast at Caesars' buffet.

We finished eating and went for a stroll past the early morning gamblers in the casino and into a long indoor mall with shops on either side of the corridor. Hardly a mall, and not at all just "shops." More like expensive boutiques—Carina, Gavril, Bernini Couture—all of it way beyond anything we could afford to spend. We needed something more like a shopping mall with a Nordstrom, a Macy's at least. It's true I wanted to spend as much of the money as I could, but I really wasn't ready to spend it all in one store. That's the kind of shopping they had at Caesars Palace.

We drove on the Strip to a place called Fashion Show Mall. Now, this was more like it. They didn't have a Macy's, which is my favorite department store, but they did have a Dillard's, a Bullock's and a Neiman Marcus. Not exactly what we were looking for, but close. I wish we had a Macy's in Santa Cruz. All we've got on the downtown Mall are Ford's and Gottschalks. There's a J.C. Penney out at Capitola Mall, but none of those come close to any of the stores in the Fashion Show Mall. The entrance where we went in led straight to a Bullock's, so that's where we went first.

"My mom used to take me to the Bullock's store in downtown Los Angeles when I was a little girl," I said. "I remember how much fun it was. The store was so fancy in those days, and downtown was always fun to go to."

"City of Paris in San Francisco was where we went when my mother wanted to take us someplace fancy. That was a lot of fun, too."

"Wow," I said as we looked at some very expensive blouses in the Bullock's store. "This is a heck of a lot more expensive than Macy's at Valley Fair."

"Yes," Danielle said with just as much enthusiasm as when she said no in that skeptical way she had. Then our conversation turned to more personal matters.

Jerome Arthur

"Pretty amazing how Mel just up and left Nora, don't you think? Running off with his secretary like that!" I said.

"Yes indeed, it *was!*"

Mel was the school principal when Danielle was my aide. The school board literally ran him out. They wouldn't give him a third four-year contract, so he got the principal's job at Cypress Elementary up in the hills above town. He was only there for about three years when he ran off to Northern California with his school secretary. It was a big scandal.

"You know, Nora had a drinking problem," I said.

"I could tell. Every year at the Christmas party, I thought she went overboard with the drinks. But she was such a nice lady, and I think he should've worked harder at the relationship. Should've got her into a program, A.A., Janus, something."

"Easier said than done. My dad's an alcoholic. Mom and I never could get him to admit that he was. She went to her grave never hearing him admit it. And that's the first step. You've got to admit that you've

61

got a drinking problem before you can start dealing with it. He's still drinking. Soc's dad was a worse alcoholic than mine. At least my dad made it through a thirty-five year career with the same company. Soc's dad probably didn't work twenty-five years his whole life, and that was for a lot of different companies. He was really young when he died. His dad's dad and his brother too. It's one of the reasons he doesn't drink himself, except for the occasional glass of wine."

"I sure got lucky. My Jason's only vice is technology. A real computer geek. He gives me plenty of attention and affection, though. No drugs, maybe a joint every once in a while, and definitely no alcohol."

"Same with Soc. I'm the one who was a cigarette smoker. Ten years. I started in college. They don't do this anymore, but when I was in school, they used to pass out cigarettes when you were standing in line at the admissions office or the book store. They even used to allow smoking in the classroom. Crazy huh?"

"Really crazy. They didn't know then all they know now about the health hazards from tobacco. Or they knew and weren't telling us."

"I'm thinking it was more like they knew and were hiding it," I said. "They even had T.V. ads with actors dressed in white smocks to make 'em look like doctors. 'I smoke mentholated Kools,' they'd say, as if Kools were good for your health."

"I've never smoked."

"You and Soc."

We went into separate changing rooms and tried on some of the clothes we later bought. After we made the purchases, we hung around the Mall for two more hours, window shopping mostly. We each spent a couple hundred dollars. I bought two darling blouses with floral patterns, one salmon and one light blue, and a pair of navy slacks. We had lunch at a pizza restaurant on the first floor. Since Danielle was doing me a huge favor by coming with me, I tried to pay her expenses for things, so I paid the bill for our lunch. I'd paid for all of her meals so far and was going to keep doing it. When we got tired, we went back to the time-share.

Seven

We were both pretty tired after the time we spent at the Fashion Show Mall, so we lay down and napped for a while. I was up before Danielle, so I started writing on the postcards I'd bought at the Mall. One to Caroline, one to LaVerne and one to Betty. Danielle woke up just as I finished with Betty's. I put away the five that I was sending to some of the other teachers and aides at school. We drank the bottled waters that were provided in the timeshare as we got into our bathing suits. We got towels out, put on sunscreen and wide brim hats, and went down to the pool. I put the three postcards in the mail as we passed through the lobby.

It was a really hot June afternoon. I saw a thermometer on the Strip on our way back to the timeshare that said it was over a hundred degrees. The pool and the decks all around it were crowded with nubile young women, and handsome young men. All the umbrella tables were occupied. There were some chaise lounges available, but they weren't shaded, and I wasn't going to sit out in direct sunlight. My Irish skin freckled, even with sunscreen, whenever I did that.

"Hey, Jayne!" someone shouted from the pool. When I turned to look, I could see it was the older one of the two young men we'd met the night before.

"Oh, hi," I said. I couldn't remember his name. I never was very good at remembering people's names, and I think he could see that as he said,

"It's Chad. Remember, last night?"

"Oh, right. Hi, Chad."

He could see that we were looking for someplace in the shade.

"Say, why don't you ladies go over and have a seat at our table?" he said pointing at one of the umbrella tables with towels draped over two of the chairs. He moved to the edge of the pool, got out and joined us as we sat down in the shade of the umbrella. "So, how've yuh been?" He was towel drying his hair.

"Fine," Danielle and I said, almost in unison.

"We found a mall up the street and had a great time shopping," I said.

"Just got back a little while ago," Danielle said.

"Great!"

"What've *you* been doing?"

"Not much. Mostly just hanging around here." He extended his tanned arm toward the pool. "This'll be our last night here, so we've just been relaxing. Jerry's doin' laps again."

"Yuh know, I think I'll join him," Danielle said as she stood up and dropped her towel on the chair. "It's hot out here! Even in the shade."

"Water's nice," Chad said as she walked over to poolside and went down the steps at the shallow end. Then he turned to me and said, "When're you guys headin' back to Santa Cruz?"

Jerome Arthur

"Not for a while. We're going to San Diego from here. Then it'll be on to Baja California."

"R'illy? That's cool." The expression on his face told me he was impressed with Baja. "Wha'cha goin' down there for?"

"You sound like my husband. It's one of his favorite places. He's there right now, and we're on our way to join him."

I really didn't want to share my personal business with this young man, but he was such a nice guy (he *did* remind me of Soc, not his looks so much, but his mannerisms and the way he talked), and I felt like I needed to unload on someone who knew nothing about it, so, true to form, I unloaded on poor Chad. I didn't tell him everything. I wasn't ready to go that far. I told him about Soc reading his own obituary, and how when he tried to get it straightened out, he couldn't. I didn't tell him Soc had snuck out on me, rather he'd let me know he was leaving, but only for a vacation, and that he'd planned to come home when it was over. I also didn't tell him about the note Soc left me, and the insurance.

"Big drag what happened to 'im!" he said. "I don't blame 'im for bailin', 'cept how could he do that to you? I mean, I know I haven't known you long, but you seem like such a nice lady."

"What a sweet thing to say." It was all I could think of at that moment. "It's really not like he just up and disappeared on me," I lied. "He just said he needed to get away for a while. I know where he is."

"Where's 'zat?"

"Santa Rosalillita. He's got his board and wetsuit. He says the surfing's good there."

"So, is he expecting you to be dropping in on him?"

The question told me that he knew I was withholding information from him, that he knew I wasn't telling him everything there was to tell. He seemed to be very perceptive. Even though I thought he probably knew these things, I still couldn't bring myself to discuss them with him.

"Well, not exactly, but I'm sure he'll be glad to see me when we get there."

Chad was looking skeptical, like he knew I wasn't being completely honest with him, so I suggested we join Danielle and Jerry in the water. That was the best I could do to change the subject. Plus, the heat was really getting to me, and my prevaricating wasn't helping my perspiration level one bit.

We stayed in the water long enough to get cooled down. Chad did a few dives. Danielle and Jerry got out before me, and were sitting at the table. I watched from the pool as Chad did his dives. He surely did have a beautiful, young and tanned body, and he really was a good diver. When we got out of the pool, we joined Jerry and Danielle back at the table. We were only there for a little while longer when Chad suggested that they take us out to dinner.

"They got a great spread at El Cortez on Fremont Street downtown. Great atmosphere, too. Art Deco interior design like the way they used to do it in the fifties. Wha'da yuh say? Wan'a go?"

"Sounds great!" Danielle said before I even had a chance to open my mouth. "Where and when you wan'a meet?"

69

The Finale of Seem

"R'illy? You game too?" Chad said to me.

How could I resist the way he asked his second question? That's the way Soc would've said it. How I missed that man. I should've been angry with him, and I was, but I was also longing for his return.

"Sure. It'll be fun."

We set a time, seven o'clock. The location for our third meeting would be right there at poolside. We went our separate ways back to our rooms. It was about an hour and a half before we were to meet. Danielle and I finished doing our postcards, and then we took showers and started getting ready for our double date with two brothers who were possibly young enough to be my kids. We still didn't know how old they were, but I was betting on them, certainly the younger one of the two, not being too much older than Caroline.

"So, wha'da yuh think about this?" Danielle asked as we put on make-up in the twin mirrors in the bathroom.

"What do you mean?" I knew darn well what she meant.

"You know. Goin' out on a dinner date with strangers. Young strangers to boot. I mean, the propriety of it all."

"Oh, I don't know. You were pretty prompt in your response to Chad down at the pool. Maybe we should've been a little harder to get. It's okay. We'll have a good time."

"I know we will."

Eight

The boys were at the pool when we arrived. We walked to their car, drove up Las Vegas Boulevard to Fremont Street, and parked in El Cortez Hotel/Casino's parking structure. As we walked through the casino to the Flame Steakhouse, I could see why they referred to this as "Old-style Las Vegas." It was nothing like Caesars. No wonder Chad liked the ambience.

We were seated right away. It was Tuesday night, which I was learning was the slow time in Las Vegas. Special rates Sunday through Wednesday everywhere in town, and the crowds were thinner. The Flame was by no means filled up, maybe half.

"So, what do you guys do in Pasadena?" Danielle said after we were seated in a booth.

"We're both swimming coaches and P.E. teachers. I'm at John Muir High. Jerry and I both graduated from there. Jerry went ahead and got a master's degree and a J.C. credential, so he's at P.C.C. We graduated from there, too."

"We're almost twins, yuh know," Jerry said.

"What do you mean, almost?" Danielle said. "Isn't that kinda' like being almost pregnant?"

"We're only thirteen months apart, and I skipped a grade in grammar school, so we were at the same grade level all the way through school."

"We swam for two years at P.C.C. Went to San José State as juniors. Did those two years at the Santa Clara Swim Club."

"Now we're just a couple a' old crewcut P.E. teachers with whistles hanging around our necks."

"Hardly old," Danielle put in.

The Finale of Seem

I was letting her carry the conversation. I'd already told Chad too much about my personal life.

"Compared to a couple of old broads like Jayne and me, believe me, you're both young whipper snappers," she said good naturedly.

"I think you'll be surprised when you find out how old we are," Jerry said. "We're always getting carded, and people just generally don't believe us when we tell them our ages."

"Have you guys been in Pasadena your whole lives?" Danielle said as we sipped our wine and waited for our dinners to be served.

"Born and raised," was Chad's reply.

"You said you're always getting carded. How old are you?"

"Chad's thirty-five and I'm thirty-four."

"Boy, you *do* look younger than that," Danielle said. "You're only nine years younger than me."

"See, what'd I tell yuh?"

Jerome Arthur

Neither of them asked me how old I was, and I didn't volunteer the information. Chad already knew my age and more about me than I cared for him to know, and I think he was well aware that I wasn't being completely honest with him. He seemed like a perceptive young man, and I liked him. He was a nice guy, but I didn't care if he could see how insecure I actually was. Like why was I even going looking for Soc? I was having a hard time answering that question to my own satisfaction. In a phrase, unsure of myself, and I don't really know why.

"You guys play any poker?" Danielle asked.

"You kiddin'? We been playing since high school. 'Fact we were a pretty good team when we were at San José State."

"Great! I found someone to play with. Jayne'll only play canasta with me."

"That's right," I said. "Poker players are too serious for my taste. When I play cards, I like to have fun."

"They got some good games at the Golden Nugget," Chad said. "We should check it out."

The Finale of Seem

"Let's," Danielle said.

We chatted over dinner for the next hour. When we finished, we went through the casino out onto Fremont Street. It was fairly crowded for a slow day. I guessed that street was busy all the time. We strolled up the avenue and into the Golden Nugget. A great big dollar slot machine greeted us as we entered. It was all lit up, and a big sign with flashing lights all around across the top said, "JACKPOT $550,000!" We walked through the casino past nickel, dime, quarter and fifty cent slot machines, past blackjack, roulette and craps tables. Off to the left was a room with a half-dozen or so tables with poker players sitting around them. Danielle, Chad and Jerry sat down at one that had three other players.

"Listen, I'm go'n'a go back out on the street, maybe do some shopping," I said. "When should I come back?"

"About two hours," Danielle said. "I don't want to hang around here much longer than that."

"See you then," I said and went back out through the casino to the street.

Jerome Arthur

I went into the first curio shop I came to, picked up some more postcards and browsed through some of the other nicknacks and souvenirs in the shop. Then I went back out and wandered up to the Golden Gate Casino at the end of Fremont Street and started down the other side. I stopped in a couple more gift shops.

It was full dark now, and this street was a wonderland of lights. It could have been broad daylight, but I knew better because it was getting on to nighttime when we left the timeshare, and if I looked straight up, I could see the sky was black. There was a full moon, but I couldn't see any stars because the lights were so bright. And if Tuesday was a slow day, I'd hate to be there on a busy one. There were people everywhere, on the street and in the shops and casinos. I wandered in and out of casinos all along the way. They were all open to the sidewalk, and it was kind of refreshing to get that blast of cool air in that open area between the sidewalk and the casino interior.

When I got back to the Golden Nugget, I still had another half hour before I had to meet Danielle and the boys. I stepped in and was looking at that great big slot machine we'd passed earlier. I moved around the casino floor watching a couple of black-jack games and the roulette wheel. Then I saw an older woman get a jackpot on one of the quarter slot machines. I'm not sure if that was what prompted me to do what I was about to do, or if it was just a whim, but whatever it was, I decided to get ten silver dollars, no more, and put them in the big slot machine out in front and try my luck.

I walked over to the cashier and changed a ten dollar bill. Then I went back to the slot machine and dropped the silver dollars, one at a time, in the coin slot. After each one, I pressed the button and stood back. I dropped three silver dollars in the slot and got nothing. As I dropped the fourth one in, I thought I was wasting my time and money. I really didn't have any expectations when I changed the ten dollar bill. Well, the fourth turned out to be the charm. It seemed like the cylinders turned a long time before they finally came to a stop, and when they did, I saw five sevens lined up evenly in the window. And then, to my astonishment, within five seconds, bells and whistles started to sound, and the screen that said, "JACKPOT $550,000!" started to flash with the lights around it.

This was unbelievable! Amazing! I let out a scream of joy. I think I might've jumped up, too. I couldn't tell because suddenly the details of the event became very fuzzy. I felt like I was dreaming. All of the sounds around me—the slot machines, the low hum of groups of people talking over craps and roulette—were silent. I felt dizzy, but not enough to lose my balance or pass out. I was in a trance but I was wide awake.

Nine

I stood frozen in front of that slot machine. Slowly, the casino sounds started to re-enter my consciousness. I couldn't believe it. Things like that never happened to me. I couldn't move, and then suddenly a crowd gathered around the machine and me, and they all started cheering and applauding. Then a smiling casino employee wearing a double-breasted, pinstriped suit appeared, it seemed, out of nowhere.

"Good evening, ma'am. I'm Herb Jones representing Golden Nugget Las Vegas. Congratulations! That's quite a jackpot you've won there!"

"Indeed it is," I managed to say without tripping over my words. I was speechless. My heart was pounding. People were still crowded around me. It seemed they wanted to be close to me, like maybe whatever luck I'd had would rub off on them. It was a strange mirage of a scene.

"May I see a picture I.D. We'll try to expedite this as quickly as possible."

I fumbled around in my purse looking for my wallet. My hands were trembling. It was the biggest thing that ever happened to me. It hardly seemed worth the effort to show I.D., as he only gave my California driver's license a cursory glance and returned it to me. When he spoke next, I realized that he was only looking to see what my name was.

"Well, Ms. Smith, if you would accompany me to my office, we'll pay out your winnings. If you'll just follow me," he said and started to move off.

"Wait. I've got some friends playing poker over there," I said, pointing at the room where they were.

"All right, Ms. Smith," he said extending his hand and following my lead.

When we got there, Danielle was playing with only two other players. Chad and Jerry were standing near the entrance, watching.

"What's happening?" I said as I approached. "Why aren't you two playing?"

"Too rich for our blood," Chad said. "Danielle started off by winning five straight hands. Built up a real nest egg. Then she lost a couple, and now she's on another roll. Got'a be up ten thousand, 'least five. Those two guys she's playing with 're a couple high rollers. She's good! Better player than them."

Herb Jones stood by patiently as I had this exchange with Chad, but I could see that he was wanting to get me to his office, so I quickly told the boys what I'd won and how I'd won it. They started asking me questions, and I held a hand up to silence them.

"How long will this take?" I asked Herb.

"Shouldn't take more than about a half hour. Maybe forty-five minutes."

I turned to the two boys and told them to tell Danielle what was happening, and that I'd meet them back here in about forty-five minutes. Then I followed Herb Jones to his office. It was an unbelievably simple transaction. After he got the fax all set up, the only thing I had to do was type in the account number of a savings account we had. I had the passbook in my purse. That money matched everything we had in the closet ($25,000) before Soc left with ten of it, and I brought the other fifteen with me in travelers checks. Just as soon as I typed in the number, we would have about four hundred thousand dollars in that account. That was after Uncle Sam and the Governor's office took theirs. It boggled my mind.

When I got back to Danielle and the brothers, I felt like I was walking in the clouds. I still thought it was all a dream. I was starting to have conflicting feelings about Soc. It was funny how I hadn't thought about him in a while. I was thinking of maybe ending the trip, taking the money and running, not away, but back home. Leave Soc to his devices. The more I thought about it, the more I realized that I just couldn't bring myself to go through with a plan like that. Who knew why, but I really did love Soc, and I wanted him back.

The Finale of Seem

"So, how much did you end up winning?" I asked Danielle, breathlessly. "Chad said you were ahead when I talked to him."

"Forget about my winnings! What about yours? Those boys said you won a half a million dollars! That right?"

"That's right! So exciting! I thought I was going to pass out there for a minute! I still think it's a dream, and when I wake up, it'll all be gone. Tell me I'm wrong. How about you? Did you end up winning?"

"As a matter of fact, I did." Her usual enthusiasm turned to uncharacteristic composure. She got very calm and cool. "Yes, I did really well. Lucky to've gotten into a game with a couple testosterone-driven high rollers who weren't very good stud poker players. Like taking candy from a baby. I think they were pissed mostly because I'm a woman. You can't win at poker when you let stuff like that get in your way. They thought I would be easy pickings. I won seven thousand and some change. Don't know which one took the worse beating. Not my problem."

"Boy, you ladies broke the bank in Vegas! Not everyday that happens," Chad said.

We got back to the timeshare about eleven-thirty, and because we were all (especially Danielle and I) so excited that we couldn't sleep, we decided to go for another moonlight swim. We met back at the pool at a little before midnight, and were the only ones there. The temperature was still in the nineties. It felt so good to get in the water. Chad started diving; Jerry was doing his laps; Danielle and I splashed around a little and got out. I noticed that the boys were treating us differently since we'd won all that money. They seemed a little more standoffish, a little less flirtatious, and that was all right with me, but I just wondered why. Maybe now we intimidated them. We said goodbye to them at the pool and went back to our room.

The enormity of what just happened to both of us hadn't hit me yet. Danielle was as cool as a cucumber. Of course this wasn't the first time she'd ever gambled and won. She had the timeshare in Las Vegas, and visited Tahoe a couple times a year. This was a virgin rush for me. We talked some before we fell asleep.

"You notice how sheepish the brothers got after we won the money?"

"Yes. I think I freaked them out when I talked about the two high rollers. I think they might be afraid I'll break their balls like I supposedly did to those other two."

"I think you're right. I also think our lives are never going to be the same again. Like staying in the place we're going to tomorrow? You know what I'm talking about? You know about the Hotel del?"

"Not really," said Danielle. "I've heard of it, but that's all."

"I've always wanted to spend a night there, but never thought I could afford it. Well, now I can. It's where most of the movie *Some Like It Hot* was filmed. You ever see it?"

"Great movie."

"It's probably Caroline's favorite movie. She's a big Marilyn Monroe fan. My mother-in-law's job was in San Diego the last few years before she retired. We visited her a couple times, and she took us down to the Hotel del. Caroline was enchanted as we walked along the same beach that Marilyn Monroe and Jack Lemon cavorted on in the movie. She's a big Jack Lemon fan, too."

We talked like that for half an hour before we fell asleep. I had sweet dreams of paying off our mortgage and paying cash for a new car. It was a lot better dream than the one I'd had the night before.

Ten

For as late as it was that we got to sleep, we were awake at seven o'clock. The first thing I did was call Caroline to tell her about my jackpot and Danielle's good luck, and of course skill, at playing cards. I told her where we were staying that night. I wanted to get moving, not spend a lot of time on the phone, but Caroline wanted to ask me a lot of questions, mostly about the windfall, but she also told me how jealous she was because we were staying at the Hotel del that night. I told her there'd be plenty of time later to talk about it all. Right at that moment, I wanted to get moving, so I said I'd call her from San Diego.

We wasted no time getting packed and ready to leave. We didn't see Chad and

Jerry again when we checked out at eight the next morning. We crossed the Strip to the Stardust and went to the buffet breakfast there. We filled the gas tank on our way out of town, and we were on I-15 by nine-thirty. It was a little before noon when we got to Barstow, so that's where we had lunch. We found a fifties-style diner similar to the one in Paso Robles. There wasn't much in the way of tourist attractions in Barstow, so we got right back on the road to San Bernardino and points south.

The temperature got a little cooler as we came down the mountain into San Bernardino, the key words, of course, being "a little." I saw a time and temperature sign at a car dealer that said it was eighty-one degrees.

"Know what people around here call this place?" I said.

Danielle had been driving since Barstow.

"You mean San Bernardino?"

"Yeah, locals call it Berdoo."

"Isn't *that* a strange thing to call a town?"

"I suppose."

89

The Finale of Seem

When we got to Riverside we branched off on I-215 and that took us down through Perris and Sun City to Temecula back on I-15.

"Wow!" I said. "I'm having a real blast from the past here."

"Really! Pray tell!"

"Soc and I came out here a couple times the first year we were married. We knew we wanted to move out of the Los Angeles area, and this was one of the places we came to and looked at."

"That how you found Santa Cruz?"

"Yes. In fact coming out here helped us decide to stay near the coast. This convinced us we didn't want to move inland. The first time we were on an overnight camping trip with two other couples. They both had Jeeps and all we had was a Volkswagen station wagon."

"You mean a bus?"

"No. It was a station wagon. Soc used to call it a square back."

"I remember those."

"Yeah, well anyway, the two couples we were with came here a couple weekends a month, what they called four-wheeling. They really knew their way around the desert. We weren't able to leave Long Beach till later in the day because Soc worked Saturdays, so we met them that evening at the Long Branch Saloon up ahead in Temecula. They were here earlier in the day doing their four-wheeling all afternoon. We had hamburgers and beers at the bar; then we went to a place called Ocotillo Wells by the Salton Sea. We slept under the stars on a sand dune. It was lovely. The moon was full and there were a million stars out. Did you notice how you could hardly see the stars last night in Las Vegas?"

"Oh, yes. First thing I noticed night before last as soon as we got out of the car at the timeshare. I'm aware of it every time Jason and I go there. Don't forget, we live in the Santa Cruz Mountains. You can see the stars every night. Nothing like Las Vegas."

"That's the way it was that night in Ocotillo Wells. You could see the Milky Way. It was so beautiful."

"You want me to pull off the freeway at Temecula?" Danielle asked.

The Finale of Seem

"Sure. We've got time. It'll be kinda' fun to see how much the place has changed."

As we pulled into town, I could see how different things were since Soc and I had been there all those years ago. I remembered it looking like an old west town with the Long Branch right at the center. Now there were housing tracks and shopping centers everywhere. There was hardly any open space between Temecula and Murrieta. It was like Los Angeles and Orange County. When I was a little girl, a drive to Orange County was a drive to the country. I went to Disneyland the first year it opened, and there was nothing from Norwalk to Anaheim. Just wide open spaces and a lot of orange groves.

Eleven

We didn't stop in Temecula. We got right back on I-15 and went straight through Escondido and on to San Diego. We arrived at the Hotel del Coronado at three-thirty. It was a huge wooden building (complex was more like it) sitting right on the beach. It seemed bigger than I remembered it, but I knew it wasn't. After we got registered, we walked through the lobby to the veranda that faced the beach. We took in the view. There were still quite a few sunbathers on the beach, and sitting in deck chairs on the veranda were a very attractive looking man by himself, and a couple basking in the afternoon sun. We went back into the lobby where the bellhop waited next to our luggage. He showed us to our rooms.

The Finale of Seem

"Wow, what a nice suite!" I said as we walked in.

"I'll say!" Danielle echoed my enthusiasm.

"And what makes it extra special is I don't have to worry about how much it costs."

And since now money was no object, I had called from Las Vegas and upgraded our reservation from a room to one of their most expensive suites, what they called a Resort Suite. I didn't care how much it cost. I could've easily spent the whole fifteen thousand dollars I had in traveler's checks on that suite, but I didn't have to because it wasn't that expensive. The room was like no other I'd ever seen before. Clean and plush. Just like in the movie. This was the lap of luxury. As we stepped into the suite, we were looking straight across the room at the French doors leading to a balcony with sweeping ocean views.

"Oh, my!" Danielle said as she walked over, opened the doors and stepped out.

"Pretty amazing, huh?" I said.

I followed her out and we both took in the fantastic view. The bellhop moved our suitcases in, put them on luggage stands, and stood by the exit door.

"Is there anything else I can get for you ladies?" he asked.

"I think we're fine," I replied.

As I approached him, I opened my purse and took my wallet out. The smallest change I had was a twenty dollar bill. Not even thinking twice about it, I handed him the money and thanked him.

"Thank *you*, ma'am! You just let me know if there's anything I can get you!"

He bowed and took his leave. I was absolutely flabbergasted at the change in my life just since last night. I liked it! The kind of treatment we were getting was positively delightful. Danielle was enjoying it, too. After we got settled in, we both plopped down on the king size bed and took short naps.

When we awoke, we freshened up and went down to the ground floor where the shops were all around in the main part of the hotel. There were clothing boutiques and gift shops, but the one that caught my eye was something called Est. 1888. It was a history-of-the-Hotel-del store. There were books on sale that chronicled the hotel's past, and they had other artifacts that represented various periods in the hotel's history. They had a lot of gift items, like stuff that had to do with *Some Like It Hot*, and other movies and books that used the hotel for their settings. I bought Caroline a big coffee table book that had lots of great pictures of scenes from the movie and the complete movie script. I knew she'd like that. There were historic artifacts all over the store. It was great! I bought some postcards that showed various stages of construction in 1887 and 1888 and others over the years during the hotel's existence. It had just celebrated its hundredth anniversary the year before. It was my kind of shop. Neither Danielle nor I was much interested in stores like Isabel B., although we did look at and admire the high quality clothes, shoes and accessories they had. It was quite nice. Danielle bought some Crabtree & Evelyn bath products from a store called The Sea Bath & Body. The fragrances in that store were unbelievably luscious.

We went to the Sheerwater and made dinner reservations for seven-thirty on the terrace. From there we took our purchases to our suite, and then we went down to the beach and walked along the shoreline. It was getting late in the day. The sun was moving toward the horizon, but we still had lots of daylight. We were within a few days of the longest day of the year. It was a lovely walk.

The soft, wet sand was squishing between my toes, a feeling I've always liked. The beach wasn't crowded at that hour. A couple of people were building very elaborate sand castles. On one side of us, we could see the open ocean, and on the other the majestic old wooden Victorian building that was the hotel.

"'Afternoon," said a gentleman who passed us on the sand.

We greeted him and he went on his way.

"Wow!" said Danielle. "What a good looking man!"

"Yes, he is," I said. "'Member seeing him on the veranda when we first got here?"

"No. When was that?"

"He was one of the people sitting in a deck chair on the veranda when we walked through the hotel right after we checked in."

"Oh, I remember now. He was sitting by himself. There was a couple there, too."

"Right."

He was a distinguished looking gentleman (my age, maybe a little younger, but definitely not looking it) with dark hair graying at the temples. He wore baggy shorts and a T-shirt. It was obvious he was a weight lifter, but not overdone. Definitely not muscle bound, just standing straight up with dark chiseled features and broad muscular shoulders. I could tell he was no spring chicken, though he *looked* more like Danielle's age than mine. He was so striking, in fact, that I had to do a double take, and when I did, I saw him looking our way.

We walked for another fifteen minutes and then headed back to the hotel. We got to the suite at six o'clock. Danielle lay down and took a short nap, and I started doing my postcards to Caroline, LaVerne and Betty. I also included Rick, the second grade teacher and the only man on our staff. He was my buddy. Danielle awoke as I was finishing writing my postcards. We started getting ready for our seven-thirty dinner reservation.

Twelve

We arrived at the restaurant five minutes before our reservation and were seated at the outer edge of the terrace next to two palm trees. An expansive, palm tree-dotted lawn stretched out to a hedge that separated the beach from the hotel grounds. Beyond the hedge were views of San Diego Bay and the Pacific Ocean. A point poked out and separated the two views. A few minutes after we took our seats, the sun went down behind the point.

"What's that point called," I asked the waiter when he came to take our drink order.

"Point Loma. National monument out there. Cabrillo National Monument."

"Is it a good place to surf?"

"You bet. Good point break. You surf?"

"No, but my husband does. A real fanatic. You look like you might be a surfer."

He fit the role well. He was a real towhead; his sun bleached hair was a contrast to his tanned face.

"No doubt," he replied. "'Fact I went out today. May I get you ladies something from the bar while you view the menu?"

"I'll have a glass of the house white wine," said Danielle.

"And I'll have red."

As we waited for our drinks, we looked around the terrace and into the restaurant. It was maybe half-full with diners. Judging the crowd, I'd say that the Sheerwater was probably a popular place for locals. It looked like perhaps only half the people there were staying at the hotel. There was only one other table with two women. All the others were either occupied by a man and a woman, or two couples. There was one table with three couples.

The waiter brought our drinks and we ordered. As he walked away from our table, I noticed the good looking gentleman we'd seen earlier being escorted by the maître d' to a table-for-two on the other side of the terrace. We were directly in the line of his view of the beach. I thought because he was looking our way, he was merely taking in the view, but I soon realized that he was indeed watching us. At one point he caught my glance in his direction. He stood up and walked our way.

"Oh, God! What's this?" I said to Danielle under my breath.

"Hi, I'm Maxwell Shane," he said, extending his right hand when he got to our table. "My friends call me Max. And you are?"

I was so taken aback that I hesitated to reply. He was looking at me and addressing me only. I really didn't want to give him my name. I had this eerie feeling about the man. He was too forward and too smooth for my liking. And way too handsome. I was trying to avoid his question. I thought about the summer between junior and senior year in college when I went to Europe by myself. I remembered the time in Rome when I was

102

riding on a streetcar and some young Casanova came up to me and started groping me and talking to me in Italian. I didn't understand a word he said, but I knew by his fresh behavior that he was up to no good. I started signing, pretending I was a deaf mute, and he moved away from me quicker than he approached. I knew that tactic wouldn't work with the handsome man at the Hotel del, and I really didn't know what else to do. If we were playing a chess match, I'd be in check.

"Jayne," I said, offering him my hand. I was careful not to give him my full name. He had a firm handshake that seemed to exude confidence. And then to bring Danielle into the conversation, I introduced her also by first name only.

"You know, I was just wondering if I could join you ladies for dinner. It's really not much fun dining alone."

I looked at Danielle, but she wasn't giving me any clues as to how she felt, so I made a snap decision and invited him to be seated. Who knew? Maybe I had misjudged him because of my first impression. He sat in the chair next to Danielle and stared straight at me. I was unsure about his dark eyes. His seeming confidence in himself was palpable. Something about him. I just didn't know. He didn't seem vulnerable in any way. That was one thing about Soc. Sometimes he could be so exposed and helpless, and then it would be my turn to be the school teacher that I am, to take charge and bring him through

"Are you ladies staying in the hotel?" he asked looking at me.

"Yes," I replied. "You?"

At the moment I wasn't going to be any more informative or inquisitive.

"Oh, yeah. I always stay here when I'm in San Diego. 'Bit pricey, but well worth it. Ever stay here before?"

"No. I've only ever *been* here a couple of times. My daughter's a fan of the movie *Some Like It Hot*. My husband and I brought her here a couple of times when she was a teenager."

I was hoping the information I was giving him would be a turnoff. How many guys would seriously pursue a married woman with a grown daughter? I was learning as the years passed that there were many.

And, as it turned out, Max was one of them. He soldiered on.

"How old's your daughter now?"

"Twenty-two her next birthday."

"And I imagine she's just as pretty as you."

So, there it was, the first run, and Danielle wasn't helping.

"She is a beautiful girl in her own right," she said.

"I'll *b*et," he said, putting extra stress on the b, and not taking his eyes away from mine. "How long have you ladies been friends?"

He'd finally turned his gaze to Danielle when he said this.

"Long time," she said. "Ten years maybe. I used to be her classroom aide. Now I've got my own classroom."

"Ah, so you ladies are teachers?"

"That's right."

Now she was helping by taking the focus from me. Also, because she was a lot more blunt than I was, she had a no-nonsense air about her, and he seemed to sense it and be somewhat impressed by it. The jousting

105

went on for the rest of the evening. This guy's line was as smooth as his looks, but Danielle was holding her own. Her style was a little rougher than Max's, but that roughness held her in good stead. They talked about everything in art from the French impressionists to Macedonian architecture, in music from Beethoven to the Beatles, in literature from Mark Twain to John Steinbeck. They covered the gamut. I threw in my two cents worth when they were talking about something I knew, like the Beatles.

The conversation went on through dinner and into dessert, which I usually didn't order, but this time did because of my new wealth and an attitude that I didn't care anymore if I gained weight, which I knew I wouldn't because I had such good metabolism. There was just something on Max's side that wasn't computing with me. I had an uneasy feeling about him and everything he talked about. Too slick. We didn't leave the restaurant till almost nine-thirty. That's how much we were talking.

"Would you ladies like to have a nightcap in the bar?" he said after he picked up the bill and we got up to leave. "The B&S right over here is a great bar, and I'm buying."

Personally, I was ready to go to the suite and go to bed, but Danielle wanted to go for the drink. Even though I knew she could take care of herself just fine, I didn't want to leave her alone with this stranger I didn't trust, so I joined them. We sat at a table in the middle of the room. The bar was a beautiful honey-colored wood of some kind. Oak, maple, I don't know. It was stunningly gorgeous. There were ceiling fans the same shade as the bar. The rest of the place was painted off-white, and there were potted palms throughout that gave off an exotic, tropical look.

Like the Sheerwater, the B&S had a good crowd for a Wednsday night, perhaps too good for what was about to happen. Looking back on it, I think the crowd was proportionate to the embarrassment of the moment. It was indeed embarrassing for us, but it was much more than that for the man

107

we were having a drink with. We'd only had a couple of sips from our drinks when two men in rumpled suits approached our table. They both looked right at Max as one of them pulled out a wallet and flipped it open showing him a badge.

"Excuse me, sir. Are you Maxwell Shane? Maxwell Alan Shane?"

"Now, you know I am," Max replied, smiling. "How may I help you?"

"May we talk to you privately out-side?" the one with the badge said.

"May I ask what it's about?" He was still smiling.

"I think you'll want to discuss it out of the presence of the ladies, and everybody else in here for that matter."

"Oh, okay."

At this point my heart was racing, and I found out later that Danielle was having the same experience. Las Vegas all over again, but that was a heartbeat of joy. This one was brought on by anxiety and fear. What was going on? Who was this guy who'd insinuated himself into our little party? What crime had he com-mitted or been witness to?

108

I was glad the policeman suggested taking the conversation out of there. I really didn't want to know why they wanted to talk to him. He stood up and before he left, he turned a smile to Danielle and me and said,

"This is a misunderstanding. I'll be back shortly and explain. Okay?"

Then he turned and left, led by one policeman, followed by the other. And that, we thought, was the last we'd see of him, but it wasn't. Two days later we'd see him again. We finished our drinks and left the bar. Since Max had been taken away, he hadn't paid for them, so we paid and left. Everybody else in there was pretty much staring at us since he had left. They were all trying not to be too obvious about it. There was no sign of him anywhere in our walk from the bar to our suite.

"My heart's pounding!" I said as we went into the room.

"Mine too!" Danielle said. "What a harrowing experience! Wonder what he did."

"You can count on it being something sleazy. I was wary of him from when he first spoke to us. Seemed like a pretty oily character."

"I got that impression too."

The telephone on the nightstand rang. I answered it, and heard a polite male voice at the other end.

"Hello, Ms. Smith? This is Stephen, the maître d' at the Sheerwater."

"Yes?"

"I apologize for calling you like this, but we have a little problem with your bill. You see, it was paid by Mr. Shane, but it turns out Mr. Shane's credit card was rejected. When we tried to contact him for payment, we learned that he was arrested in the B&S Bar. Anyway, I regret to inform you that your and Ms. Boardain's bill has not been paid; therefore, we are requesting that you pay it."

Without hesitation, I said, "Absolutely. We were prepared to pay our bill from the start. We only invited Mr. Shane to join us after he'd ingratiated himself into our party. I will be down shortly with the money."

I hung up and explained to Danielle what had happened. No wonder he requested separate checks when we ordered. We went down together, and I paid the bill myself.

"So, what do you think that was about?" I asked Danielle when we got back to the suite.

"Don't know. I tell yuh, I've met a lota' con men and just plain smooth operators when Jason and I have taken poker trips to Vegas and Tahoe, but I've never seen a scene like what we just experienced in that bar."

"Pretty scary. I wonder what he did. Think those policemen were from the bunco squad or maybe narcotics? Maybe Max's a drug dealer. I guess we'll never find out."

"You know, that's the first bad thing that's happened to us since we've been traveling. We've had really good luck. I mean look at Las Vegas."

"Yes, indeed we have had some luck. 'Specially me. That was plain dumb luck. At least there was some skill involved with what you did. You knew how to play poker when

111

you sat down. All I did was put some coins in a slot and pressed a button."

We talked till midnight. It was good that we'd moved our conversation away from Maxwell Shane and into more pleasant subjects. It calmed us down. Our hearts weren't racing anymore. When we finally did go to bed, we were exhausted and we fell asleep right away.

Thirteen

Once again we were up early for having gone to bed so late. We went back to the Sheerwater at seven when they opened their breakfast buffet. We got on the road by eight-thirty, and we crossed the border by nine-fifteen.

It's only about a hundred and fifty miles from Tijuana to Camalú, but I was learning fast that it was no ordinary hundred and fifty miles, like what you might travel in the U.S. For one thing, it's only a two lane road from Ensenada to Camalú, and you have to be careful. On an earlier trip I learned that Mexican truck drivers handle their vans with wild abandon. Bus drivers are like that, too. You've got to be careful coming up over rises or around corners.

The Finale of Seem

Soc and I had traveled this way ten years ago. On a whim, we decided to spend New Year's Eve that year in Ensenada. We arranged for my parents to take care of Caroline while we were gone. We left from their house. I didn't have very pleasant memories of that trip. I remembered that the air in Tijuana smelled like poop. Not much had changed since then. It still smelled bad.

I didn't remember anything about the drive because Soc was behind the wheel. Now that I was driving, I was learning really fast about the speed traps and the inconsistency of speed limit signs in Tijuana. For one thing, I wasn't used to the metric system, but I did know that fifty kilometers per hour was roughly thirty miles an hour. The problem wasn't in the conversion; it was in the speed limit signs. I noticed several times in three block stretches that the speed limit changed from fifty to forty, and then back to fifty. Heading south out of town after the third time this happened, we got caught in a speed trap.

The officers in khaki uniforms had a shiny new radar gun. They must've had five cars lined up in front of us and three more behind us, and they weren't in any rush to take care of business. There were cops on the driver and passenger side of the car spending from five to ten minutes on each vehicle. When they got to the car right in front of us, I could see why it was taking so long.

"See what's going on there?" Danielle asked as we watched them deal with the driver. "Look there! See that?"

Just as she said it, I saw the driver of the car hand something to the officer.

"He's paying his fine right now. That's how they do it down here. This place is so corrupt. Let me take care of this," she said as the policeman waved us forward.

Danielle's last name before she married Jason was Chávez, and she grew up in the Mission District in San Francisco. She spoke perfect Spanish. The only Spanish I had was two years in high school and a year in college. I wasn't nearly as good as Danielle. I've always been good with punctuation and grammar, and that was no different when I was studying Spanish. I never acquired much of a vocabulary and I was only passable at conjugating verbs. Thus only a smattering of Danielle's conversation with the policeman came through.

She talked to him for at least ten minutes. I didn't understand much of it, but I could tell by her tone and mannerisms that she was simultaneously arguing with and sweet-talking the policeman, and he seemed just as simultaneously amused and annoyed at her little speech. He had an obsequious smile on his face the whole time. I thought it was taking us longer than the cars that had been ahead of us. I found it interesting that the officer on my side was talking right past me directly to Danielle once he'd determined that I couldn't speak Spanish. I understand the logic, but after all, I was the driver. Even though Danielle didn't seem concerned, I was starting to worry that there was a problem because it was taking so long. Finally, Danielle got her wallet out of her purse and handed over a twenty dollar bill to the guy on her side.

"Gracias," said the smiling officer to me as he stepped back and tipped his hat.

I put the car in gear and pulled onto the road, trying not to go over the lowest posted speed limit till we got out of town.

"What were you two talking about, and why was it taking so long?"

"We were just playing with each other. At first he said that we had to go back into Tijuana and go to court. I told him that we wanted to get to Camalú today, and if we went back into town, it might take us the rest of the day to take care of the ticket. It's already past noon."

Danielle's pronunciation of the Spanish words seemed pretty good to me. Her accent seemed just as good as the policeman's.

"Know what he said? It's unbelievable! He said it's still early in the morning. I couldn't believe it! I asked him if I could give him the fine and he could pay it for me."

"What? That's a bribe!"

"Hey, it's the only thing that works down here. And you have to put it to them that way. Like you're not trying to bribe them, but you really do want to pay your fine. You just want them to do it for you. Let's hope it doesn't happen again."

The trip from Tijuana to Ensenada went quickly, only a little over an hour. Of course, that's because it's a four lane stretch of road, and the only stops we had to make were at toll booths. It was a little different story from Ensenada to Camalú. It was about the same distance, but it took us twice as long to make the trip. The road wasn't unlike Highway 1 from Cambria to Carmel, narrow and winding. Top speed was maybe forty miles an hour; average speed was more like twenty-five or thirty. It was only a hundred and twenty mile trip, but it was slow going.

That traffic stop really slowed us down. We didn't get out of Tijuana till after noon, and then there was the two lane road. We didn't make it to Camalú till after four o'clock, and we were beat. We found the motel that Jack told us about and checked in. We moved our suitcases into the room and collapsed on the bed. We slept for a couple of hours. Since we'd spent the lunch hour bribing the cops in Tijuana, we really didn't get anything to eat all day. Good thing we ate heartily at the Sheerwater's breakfast buffet.

We got up, took showers and walked toward the center of the village where we found a little hole in the wall of a restaurant and had a couple of green chile burritos and bottled water. Danielle asked the waitress what time they opened in the morning, and she said eleven o'clock. We didn't want to stay there that long, so Danielle asked if there was any place close by that was open earlier, and she said Colonia Vicente Guerrero about fifteen miles south of there.

After dinner we went back to the motel, got into the car and drove the two miles of dirt road out to the beach. We got there before sunset and found a place to park on a bluff overlooking the beach and the ocean. It was a very different sunset than the ones we got in Santa Cruz where you could only see it set in the ocean between October and March. In Camalú it looked like it would go down in the ocean every day. The colors were similar, orange to purple to indigo. The moon was waning from full; the stars were out in profusion.

The Finale of Seem

"We should get back to the motel," I said. "It's starting to get dark, and you know, Jack did tell me that you don't want to be on the road after dark in Baja California."

"I agree with that," said Danielle.

I started the car and put it in gear. In ten minutes we were back at the motel. We didn't go to bed right away. Rather, we talked about our plan for the next morning. Looking at the map, I could see that we had just under two hundred miles to go. It looked like the road was about the same as it was from Ensenada to Camalú, so I guessed it would take us about six hours, if yesterday's drive was any measure.

"Let's not waste any time getting out of here tomorrow morning," I said. "The earlier we leave, the sooner we'll get there. I feel like just telling Soc how much money I won in Las Vegas and then walking away."

"I wouldn't blame you if you did. It's what I'd do."

"I can't bring myself to do something like that. I love Soc, and I know he loves me and didn't leave because of me. I just can't get over that he left for whatever

120

reason. No, I'm going to try to bring him home, see if we can start over. Maybe have a second honeymoon in Hawaii, now that money's no object."

"Like I said before, you're too nice, too forgiving. I'd be so pissed if I were you."

"Oh, don't worry. I'm plenty angry, and like I said before, when I bring him home, his voice might be higher than it was before."

Fourteen

We awoke the next morning just as the sun was breaking over the horizon. We'd gone to bed early for a change, and we'd gotten a full night's sleep. We didn't waste any time getting packed after we'd taken our showers. Before we left, we spread the map out on the bed to look again at our route for the day. We figured we could make Colonia Vicente Guerrero in about a half hour, maybe forty-five minutes. It wasn't that far, but the road was terrible, so it took the whole forty-five minutes. It was a much bigger town than Camalú and there was a restaurant that was open.

We sat down at a table and Danielle ordered huevos rancheros and I had chorizo con huevos. We didn't spend a whole lot of time there. We just ate and got back on the road. Danielle got behind the wheel and started driving us south out of town, on to San Quintín and Lázaro Cardenas, and that would be the last "civilization" we'd see until our return trip.

Somewhere between those two little villages and El Rosario, the S.U.V. started bouncing oddly.

"What's wrong with the car?" I asked.

"Feels like a flat tire. I'll pull over as soon as I can and check it."

"Oh, God! So far México's not been very good luck for us. What are we going to do? Can't call Triple A."

"Don't worry. If it's only a flat, I know how to change a tire."

"No kidding. Where'd you learn how to do that?"

"M' dad taught me when I was a teenager, but I already knew how to do it because I used to help him do small mechanical jobs, like rotating the tires, when I was a little girl. I can do oil changes and tune ups, too."

The Finale of Seem

I was learning a lot about Danielle on this trip. It was all very impressive. She found a place where we could get off the highway and pulled over.

"Yup. Pretty much what I thought," Danielle said as we looked at the flat front passenger side tire. "I can go ahead and put the spare on, but we're go'n'a have to go back to that gas station we saw in Colonia Vicente Guerrero and get this fixed. Looks like we might even have to get a new tire. I might've driven too far on it flat. Couldn't find a place to get off quick enough. You can see what's ahead of us. I don't want to go into that without a spare tire."

She pointed to the desert we were going into.

"I agree," I said.

She proceeded to get the jack and the spare tire out of the S.U.V. When she got the flat tire off the ground, she rotated it and showed me a pretty good size nail in it. Just as she was tightening the bolts on the spare, a newer Cadillac going north pulled up. A well dressed, good looking gentleman got out and approached. Danielle was letting the car down off the jack.

"May I be of assistance, Señoras?" he said with an accent so heavy that I could barely understand him.

He was wearing what looked like a very expensive, lightweight Italian suit and a white panama fedora. His shoes were black French toes, polished so shiny that they looked almost like my patent leather pumps.

Danielle and he had about a five minute conversation in Spanish, at the end of which he bowed and said with a smile on his face,

"Buenos días."

His smile was the same obsequious one the policeman we'd bribed had. He turned and went back to his car and drove away. Danielle kept a wary eye on him until his car disappeared over a rise.

"What did you say to him?"

"I just told him that we were fine and we didn't need any help."

"C'me on. You were talking for a good five minutes. You must've said more'n that."

The Finale of Seem

"Well, yeah. He kept insisting on lending us a hand, and I kept telling him that we didn't need it. He didn't look reputable. I mean, really. Could you see him helping us, sweat and dirt and all, change a tire in the clothes he was wearing? I don't think so. Besides, we were already done by the time he pulled up, and he could see that. I just wanted to keep him moving on, and I'm not so sure we've seen the last of him. He was a Mexican version of that smooth-talking guy we met in the hotel night before last."

"I don't think I could've picked a better traveling partner. I couldn't be safer if I were with Soc."

We drove back into Colonia Vicente Guerrero and pulled into the gas station. Danielle talked to the attendant. He said that we did need a new tire. Danielle thought that would be the safest thing to do so he went to work. The gas station was across the road from a cantina. The Cadillac we'd seen south of town was parked in front. As we waited for the new tire, the Mexican came out of the cantina, and walking alongside of him was Max Shane. Luckily, they were having an animated conversation, and neither one of them looked across the road, so they didn't see Danielle and me standing in the shade of the service bay waiting for the gas station attendant to get the new tire on. They got into the Cadillac and went north on the highway.

"So, what do you make of that?" I said.

"What I make of it is that my instincts were right when I thought that Mexican was up to no good. Either that, or, and I doubt it, Max is working undercover for the cops, and they're trying to get the goods on the Mexican, so they can lock him up. But I wouldn't bet on it."

I was learning to trust Danielle's instincts. I thought that the first thing she said about him was actually true. Max and the Mexican were doing something illegal, but then I wondered how Max had gotten out of jail, if in fact, those two guys from the night before last were really policemen. Maybe they were just another couple criminals, part of the operation, whatever that was. And no sooner did that thought go through my mind than the two "cops" from the Hotel del came out of the cantina, got into a Chevrolet and followed the Cadillac north.

After he got the new tire on the rim, the mechanic remounted it on the front wheel and put the spare back on its rack. We were on the road by one o'clock. The rest of the trip south took about five hours; there were no more mishaps. The road was a narrow two lane affair through mountains and desert all the way down, and it wasn't in the best of repair. It was a desolate country from Lázaro Cardenas to Punta Prieta, only a few scattered villages here and there and some farm land. There was an airstrip on the southern edge of Punta Prieta. It was parallel with the road, and it started less than a block away from the nearest house. About ten miles south of Punta Prieta, there were two signs on the side of the road, the first one, white with black print said, "RESPETE LA NAT-URALEZA," and the second one, green with white print said, "STA. ROSALILLITA" with an arrow pointing right.

"This is where we turn," Danielle said as we approached the crossroad. She turned right and we were soon on gravel road going west. It was then that I appreciated the fact that I'd rented the S.U.V. We bumped along at ten to fifteen miles an hour on level ground for a few miles kicking up a cloud of dust. Then we came to an opening in some hills that I knew were near the coast because, for the first time in several hours, the air smelled briny. As we made it through the valley we came to a rise where we had a panoramic view of the beach and ocean.

"So this is where he ran off to," I said as we came into the village that was nestled on the beach in a little cove.

"Not much, is it?"

And, boy, was she ever right about that. To our left just below us was a one story stucco house with assorted junk, like car parts and an old junky trailer parked off toward the beach. There were a couple of other trailers parked on the sand, but otherwise the beach was relatively clean. The azure ocean was absolutely beautiful. The swell was up and there were little waves breaking all across the strand. There were a couple surfers in the water. I wondered if Soc was one of them. The gravel road turned to dirt as we rounded the little hill to our right, and there was the rest of the town. It was like a colony or settlement. There probably weren't fifty buildings in the whole neighborhood. Only a few bungalows and trailers, and right in the middle of it all was the small white stucco church, ever present in every Mexican village we'd gone through. It was like Danielle said, "Not much."

As we went down the hill that took us into the town, I could see Soc's Woody parked over next to a beat up old trailer. Danielle parked right behind it and we got out.

"Doesn't look like anybody's home," I said. "Bet Soc is one of the surfers out there in the water."

"Yeah, I think you're right. So, what do you want to do?"

"It's too hot to wait here, and I could use something to drink. Let's go to that cantina we passed and have a beer."

"That sounds great. Let's go."

Danielle did all the talking in the cantina. She ordered us a couple Dos Equis, and since we were the only ones in there, she was able to have a conversation with the bartender. Once again, I only understood a little of what they were talking about, but I did hear her use Soc's name once, and right after she used it, the bartender said, "no, no" followed by the name Joaquín.

"We were right about the guy in the water," she said when she finished talking to the bartender. "It's Soc all right. He's going by Joaquín these days."

"I thought I heard the bartender use that name."

"You did. So, what do you want to do?"

"I don't know."

"Yuh better think of something pretty quick," she said as she got up from the barstool, walked over to the open door and looked out. "The surfers've gotten out of the water and they're coming this way."

I got up and joined her at the door. I saw two guys with surfboards, and they were close enough that I could tell that one of them was Soc, looking up the street at his car and our rented S.U.V. parked behind it. I

The Finale of Seem

stepped out into the road as he approached the cantina.

The End

2012-2019

About the Author

Jerome Arthur grew up in Los Angeles, California. He lived on the beach in Belmont Shore, a neighborhood in Long Beach, California, for nine years in the 1960s. He and his wife Janet moved to Santa Cruz, California in 1969. These three cities are the settings for his ten novels.